The Problem with Plastic

By Sally Cowan

Penny and Dad took Dustin to his tennis lesson.
Dad waved through the window.

Next, they were going to the shop to get food for dinner and snacks for the week.

Please get some muffins at the shop!

Dad picked up a plastic pack off the shelf.

“These banana and oatmeal muffins look good!” he said.

“No, Dad!” said Penny.
“We must stop getting so much stuff in plastic!”

"But Dustin wants muffins for his snack!" said Dad, looking upset.

"The problem is that plastic makes huge piles of rubbish that don't break down!" said Penny. "We discussed it at school."

Penny told Dad that plastic rubbish also pollutes our seas.

I don't want that to happen to the turtles!

“Let’s bake our own muffins,” said Penny.

“That’s a splendid plan!” said Dad.

They got butter, some eggs and a bunch of yellow bananas.

For dinner, they chose some pasta in a box and mushrooms in a paper bag.

They did not get anything in plastic packs.

At home, Penny and Dad baked a batch of sixteen muffins.

When Dustin came home from his tennis lesson, he walked into the kitchen.

CHECKING FOR MEANING

1. Why did Penny ask Dad not to buy the muffins at the shop? *(Literal)*
2. What were two problems with plastic that Penny mentioned? *(Literal)*
3. Was Dustin happy with the homemade muffins? How do you know? *(Inferential)*
4. Do you think Penny and Dad made the right decision to make muffins instead of buying them? Why? *(Evaluative)*

EXTENDING VOCABULARY

discussed	What are you doing if you are discussing something? What other word or words could the author have used instead of *discussed?*
pollutes	What is the base of the word *pollutes*? If a river is polluted, is it clean or dirty? Besides plastic, what other things could pollute a river?
splendid	What words do you know that have a similar meaning to *splendid*?

MOVING BEYOND THE TEXT

1. Making food from scratch can help reduce plastic rubbish. What are some other benefits of making food from scratch instead of buying it ready made from the supermarket?

2. Have you ever made choices that are better for the environment? What did you do? What else could you do?

3. Penny taught Dad something she learned at school. Tell me about a time that you have taught someone about something you learned at school.

4. Dustin knew that he would be hungry after his tennis lesson, so he wanted some muffins to snack on. When do you need a snack? What are some healthy snacks that you like?

TIME TO WRITE

Write some sentences on a poster to convince people to use less plastic. Explain why plastic is bad for the environment. Include suggestions for how people can reduce the amount of plastic they use.